D1648977

Eli Manning

An Unauthorized Biography

BELMONT&
BELCOURT

ISBN: 9781619840713

Table of Contents

Early Life

Elisha Nelson Manning was born January 3, 1981, in New Orleans, Louisiana. He was the last of three sons of Archie – a college quarterback and an NFL veteran – and Olivia Manning – a college homecoming queen. Given that his two older brothers, Cooper and Peyton, showed an interest in school athletics and his father, Archie was deeply entrenched in the world of professional football, it wasn't really surprising that Eli went down that road too. Archie Manning, was a college football star and NFL starter for the New Orleans Saints from 1971 to 1982. He had a couple of short stints in Houston and later Minnesota, before finally retiring after fourteen seasons, to provide commentary on the Saints' radio broadcasts.

Eli was only three years old when his father retired from the world of the NFL. Too young to remember his father play, he knew of his father's professional football life only through stories and old video footage. Seven years younger than his brother Cooper and five years younger than Peyton, Eli still enjoyed playing sports just as much as his two brothers. Birth order might have something to do with Eli's mannerisms, which were decidedly more reserved and less competitive than his older brothers.

In *Manning*, an autobiography by Archie and his second-eldest son, Peyton, Archie discusses his concern regarding the relationship he shares with his sons, particularly Eli. In the book, he talks about how he has always worried about his youngest, never feeling quite as close with Eli as he was with his other two sons. It might be due to his career, which brought him to Houston and Minnesota, or the speaking engagements he would later have. Upon his return home, Eli, a quiet and reserved child, would often ignore his father.

Eli even went so far as to "ration" the affection he would share with loved ones. Growing up, Eli differentiated himself from the rest of the family, which was always very close, giving hugs and kisses. He decided that he would only allow one kiss, on Sundays. That's it, that's all.

"I was always kind of the quiet one, the shy one," Eli observed of his childhood. "Sitting around the dinner table, Cooper kind of ran the conversation. He and Peyton and my dad were the ones who carried the conversation. Mom and I never got to do a whole lot of talking."

Mother and son shared a special bond, as the more reserved ones in the family. Plus, with his father traveling for work and his two older brothers pursuing their own athletic careers away from home, it would be Olivia and Eli who would spend time together.

Right from the beginning, Olivia saw that Eli could excel, under the right conditions. In elementary school, Eli was struggling in reading and it was very possible that he would have been held back a year. Olivia immediately dedicated herself to her son, reading patiently with him one-on-one and hiring a tutor to help him get up to speed. Before long, Eli had caught up with his grade level and was able to move on to the next grade.

Playing in High School

The boys went to the Isidore Newman private school in New Orleans, where both Peyton and Cooper became high school football stars. In 1991, Peyton was the quarterback, playing with Cooper, a receiver. The Newman team made it to the state semifinals.

Cooper, the eldest, was set to follow his father's path as a professional football player. Cooper became an all-state senior wide receiver who caught everything that came his way. He was in his prime as a muscular, 6'4", 185 pounds – certainly a force to reckon with in college. He also received a scholarship as wide receiver at the University of Mississippi (Ole Miss). In 1992, all this abruptly came to a halt with a medical diagnosis that would put an end to his athletic career.

Cooper was diagnosed with an injured ulnar nerve, a common enough injury that happens to football players. It's usually identified as numbness in the fingers and hand. He went through surgery and underwent therapy for the pain after the cast was removed. However, the pain and numbness persisted. Finally, a specialist determined that Cooper suffered from a congenital condition referred to as spinal stenosis, which is a narrowing of the spinal canal. It boiled down to plain good luck that he wasn't paralyzed in the years he was playing football, especially with all the impact to his upper body. Fortunately, neither of his younger brothers shared this condition.

Eli's brother, Peyton, went on to the University of Tennessee and a football career of his own. Peyton did exceptionally well at Tennessee, going on to become the top overall pick of the 1998 NFL draft. Eli credited his brother for helping him through the football system later, teaching him what to look out for, helping him learn from his own experiences in university and eventually, professional football.

As for Eli, he enjoyed the high school athletics program, playing basketball, baseball and football once he got to the eighth grade. Even during his early days at Newman, there was already an inkling of the football superstar he would become. As a freshman,

Manning was named the team's quarterback and in the following year, he threw 2,340 yards, made 24 touchdowns and earned all-state honors. The following year, Newman's reputation on the field as an offensive force was well-established. That year, Newman's team went 9-1 and coolly advanced to the quarter-finals of the state playoffs.

At a Crossroads

By 1998, his final year at Newman, Eli Manning had already garnered praise as one of the best high school quarterbacks in the US. Peyton's success at the University of Tennessee had brought even more attention to the Manning family and before long Eli had college coaches after him. It wasn't just his father's alma mater, University of Mississippi, but a number of other prestigious football programs looking to recruit Eli, including Florida State, Louisiana State, Virginia and Texas. Thanks to his abilities and recognizable family name, Eli Manning had his pick of any school in the United States.

During his senior year, Newman's football team secured its place at the state playoffs after making it through the regular season undefeated. However, the team lost in the quarterfinals, ending the season with an 11-1 record. Manning made the high school All-America team. *USA Today* even named him Player of the Year in Louisiana. His senior year at Newman closed with a football career that included 7,389 passing yards and an impressive 81 touchdowns.

With a strong football career in the making and a choice of top colleges available, most teenagers would find themselves at a difficult crossroads. But it would seem that Manning had quickly reduced his choices to Texas, Virginia and, his parents' alma mater, Ole Miss. After all, Manning always had lots of interests, preferring not to allow any one thing to consume his time. Even in his final year of high school, at the brink of college, he still made time to relax with friends and play basketball. His friends knew him as "Easy Eli," for his trademark laid-back attitude.

Things weren't all they seemed, of course, and the pressure of being part of an important football family takes its toll, even on the laid-back youngest son. "I was unsure of myself coming out of high school," Eli admitted. "I had doubts because of all the things that Peyton had accomplished. I didn't think I was as good as him."

During high school, Manning grew closer to his mother. With his father away for professional speaking engagements for the better part of the week, Manning and Olivia began a tradition of eating dinner out once a week, just mother and son. They had a regular lineup: Casamentos for oyster poor boy; Figaro's for pizza; and Joey K's for creole cooking and catfish. It was during this time that they were able to share things about their lives.

It's no question that mother and son shared the same quiet, reserved disposition. These dinners enabled them to bond. "I got to know more about her," Manning recalled. "She told stories about growing up or about college." No longer having to compete with his brothers to be heard, Manning developed his own voice. "It kind of helped me to get my stories out," he said.

Redshirted

Manning ended up enrolling at the University of Mississippi as a business major in 1999, where his mother, father and brother, Cooper, had attended. While it was a tough call between Texas or Virginia, David Cutcliffe's sudden appointment at University of Mississippi changed everything. Eli knew Cutcliffe as one of his brother Peyton's coaches at Tennessee for four years. Cutcliffe was credited with helping Peyton become a skilled quarterback.

"I called Eli the day I got the job," Cutcliffe recalls. "He and I had talked when I was at Tennessee, and he told me he wasn't going to Tennessee. When I got this job, I told him all bets were off. I think that was the first phone call I made." It certainly seemed like Cutcliffe had made the right call.

Although fans were looking forward to seeing their new quarterback play, Cutcliffe decided to redshirt Manning for the 1999 season. This meant that Manning could practice with the University of Mississippi Rebels, but he wasn't going to be playing in any games. Normally, most first-year players get redshirted. It gives them the opportunity to train, learn about the system and observe the games. After being redshirted, they are still eligible to play for four years.

Of course, things weren't always smooth sailing. One might have hoped that Manning would have used this time to make the transition into university life and learn to deal with the demanding academic workload, however, the freshman had other things on his schedule.

Manning was arrested on a charge of public intoxication outside his fraternity house on January 31, 2000. "I was just glad to be away from my parents," he admitted later. "I was have a great time just being a college student, probably too much fun. And I got caught. I got busted on it... It probably changed my life, that whole situation."

Cutcliffe put him on curfew and had a talk with Manning that would prove to be a pivotal moment in the athlete's life. "I asked him if he really wanted to be a big-time quarterback, or was he just here to play a little football, have a good time and get through?" Cutcliffe recounted. "And I told him to think about it before he answered."

This conversation really made Manning think about what he wanted from playing football. He realized that he genuinely wanted to be great, which then forced him to really step it up.

By 2000, Eli became an active member of the Ole Miss team. While he got to play in games, he still wasn't the team's starter. That envious position belonged to Romaro Miller, a senior. Manning was picked to play in only a few games in the regular season, completing 16 of 33 passes for a total of 169 yards, but no touchdowns.

Music City Bowl 2000

The Rebels finished off the regular season with a 7-4 record, which garnered them an invitation to the Music City Bowl in Nashville, Tennessee, against West Virginia University. Their opponents dominated the first half of the game, but Manning could only watch from the sidelines.

With the team shamefully lagging behind 49-16, coach Cutcliffe decided to put Manning on the field. After all, the game seemed like it was pretty much over by all counts. Not true. Early in the fourth quarter, Manning passed to receiver Jamie Armstrong, making a 23-yard touchdown. This was the first touchdown of Manning's college career. A mere four minutes had passed when Manning connected with Omar Rayford in the end zone, making an 18-yard score. He then threw a two-point conversion to L.J. Taylor, bringing the score to 49-38. The Rebels were back in the game.

However, the new quarterback's lack of experience would seal their fate. In the next play, Manning hurriedly threw an interception that won the game for West Virginia. This was an important learning experience for Manning, and a stunning first bowl game. "That [game] helped me a lot," Manning said. "It showed me that I can move this team and I can be a college quarterback. It also showed that to the other players. They have more respect and confidence in me."

The Eli Manning Era

The Eli Manning Era began on September 1, 2001. Miller had graduated by then and running back Deus McAllister had been drafted in the first round by New Orleans. Grant Heard, the top wide receiver was also gone. This weakened the Rebel defense considerably and meant that Manning and the rest of the offense had to carry the team. This included running back Joe Gunn, wideouts Omar Rayford and Jamie Armstrong, tight end Dough Zeigler and guard Terrence Metcalf.

The Rebels opened the season with a game against Murray State. There, Manning achieved a school-record of five touchdown passes in the second half of the game as the Rebels enjoyed a 49-14 victory. Manning finished the game completing 20 of 23 passes for 271 yards.

In the 2002 season, the Rebels experienced many of the same issues – they had a limited defense, which allowed almost 30 points a game in the year before. Things were not looking good in terms of improvement. On the offensive, there was Robert Williams and Ronald McClendon vying to replace Gunn. Metcalf had left by this time to join the Chicago Bears and Tre Stallings was an offensive lineman.

The Rebels finished the regular season at 6-6, which got them a spot against Nebraska in the Independence Bowl. They came out ahead 27-23, which was a nice way to end an average season. Eli's performance in all this was exceptional, however. In just 13 games, the quarterback passed for 3,401 yards and 21 touchdowns. Needless to say, the team counted on Manning to win games.

Late in the 2002 season, rumors circulated that Eli Manning of the University of Mississippi might come out for the NFL draft after his junior season. Coaches who had seen him play with Mississippi immediately noticed the quarterback's power and arm strength. He led his team to score, staying close, bringing his team ahead late in games.

In 2003, Manning was forced to make a tough call. Either he could declare his eligibility for the NFL draft, or return to Mississippi for his senior season. While NFL scouts believed that Manning would have certainly been one of the draft's top picks, undoubtedly securing him a multimillion-dollar contract, Manning still felt that his work at Ole Miss wasn't done yet. Manning's goal was to lead the Rebels though a victorious season and a major bowl triumph.

College Achievements

Dallas, Texas. January 2, 2004. Eli Manning plays the Cotton Bowl, one of college football's biggest bowl games with the University of Mississippi Rebels. The last time Ole Miss won a major bowl was 1970, coincidentally when Eli's father, Archie, had been the team's quarterback. This time around, the Rebels won 31-28 over Oklahoma State, due in large part to Manning's efforts.

"To come to the Cotton Bowl and have your last game with all of those guys and get out a win… is something I will always remember," Manning said. "It's been a great run." For his stellar performance in the Cotton Bowl, he was named Offensive Player of the Game.

Manning was the Rebels' quarterback for four years while at University, and achieved great things, including 10,119 passing yards (he came fifth on the SEC career list); 81 touchdown passes (third on the SEC career list); and a passer rating of 137.7 (which tied him for sixth on the SEC career list). In his senior year at the

University of Mississippi, Manning was recognized with a number of awards, which included the Maxwell Award, which honors the nation's best all-round player, the SEC Player of the Year award, the Johnny Unitas Golden Arm award, National Football Foundation and College Hall of Fame Scholar Athlete Award and the Sporting News Radio Socrates award.

Chargers or Giants?

Next on Manning's agenda was the NFL draft in April. The San Diego Chargers were looking for a quarterback and most had determined that Eli was the best passer there was, even though Ben Roethlisberger and Philip Rivers were not far behind. Another worthy contender was Tulanbe's J.P. Losman, who was then projected to be a late first rounder.

Archie Manning was working behind the scenes, trying to orchestrate the kickoff of his son's NFL career. He was worried that the Chargers were bound to be a losing team and instructed Tom Condon, Eli's agent, to tell San Diego general manager A.J. Smith to advise against taking Eli. Condon then suggested that the New York Giants would be the best match.

On draft day, Commissioner Paul Tagliabue announced the first selection. The Chargers had chosen Eli, which brought on a chorus of boos from New York fans. Philip Rivers was selected fourth overall by the New York Giants. At the press conference a few minutes later, Manning said, "Obviously, it's a great honor to be selected as a first pick in the NFL Draft. I've worked hard to be in this situation and obviously, you go into a list of a few people who have been selected first. So it is a great honor, but obviously, it's not how we wanted everything to be." Manning's disappointment on the choice was clear for everyone to see.

Surprisingly, the Chargers ended up trading Manning over to the Giants. In return, New York gave them Philip Rivers, along with their first and fifth round selections in the 2005 draft. It all happened very quickly and most New York Giants fans will agree that it was one of the strangest trades in NFL draft history.

A Giant – The Next Great Manning?

At the time, the New York Giants already had a great quarterback in Kerry Collins, but general manager Ernie Accorsi could not say no to Eli Manning, who he believed was a potential All-Pro. Scouting at one of the Rebels' games, Accorsi commented, "[Manning] was trying to do it all by himself, and he tried to force his team into the end zone when he was finally picked off. He was all over the field. Never chastised a teammate or gestured when the player dropped the ball or ran the wrong pattern."

Chris Mara, Giants' vice president of player evaluation said it wasn't just Manning's impressive statistics that caught his eye. "What stood out with him over the other guys coming out was his awareness, his ability to see the field, which is probably more a family trait. It had nothing to do with his arm, his athletic ability or that type of prowess. It was his total awareness of the game."

This translated into a six-year, $54 million contract with the New York Giants. The 23 year old managed to swing a signing bonus of

$20 million, which was the largest guaranteed bonus for a rookie in NFL history, and the second-highest of all time, just shy of Peyton's $34.5 million signing bonus, as part of a $98 million contract. Eli Manning's contract also includes $9 million in incentives.

Growing Pains

His first mini-camp was a disaster. Manning was a rookie and it showed. He fumbled snaps and missed receivers. From the get-go, Giants coach Tom Coughlin claimed the position of starting quarterback was up for grabs, but it was assumed by the beginning of training camp that two-time MVP Kurt Warner would get the gig. After all, Manning was still learning and as the Giants' playoff chances were quite slim, it didn't seem necessary to rush him along.

Manning admitted that he wasn't comfortable with the Giants' offense right away. His time in the mini-camps made that clear. They provided him with a simplified playbook a few weeks before the start of the mini-camps. Towards the end of the last camp, coach Kevin Gilbride remembers Manning was asking detailed questions like a veteran. Accorsi recalls, "He was not only changing plays out there, he was changing protections."

Things were looking up for Manning in the first few weeks of regular training camp and it seemed like Kurt Warner needed to be a little more careful. According to fullback Jim Finn, "[Manning] is making some throws where you are astounded. The other day, he put a ball 50 yards in the corner of the end zone right on the money. That's as good a throw as you can make. I don't know what Archie was doing when they were younger, but they are both unbelievable. I think Eli has the potential to do what Peyton has done, and maybe exceed it."

Super Bowl 2008

Manning's early years on the Giants taught him a lot about the animal that is professional football. He worked on his plays and racked up more yards and touchdown passes. He also stepped up and took more of a leadership role on the team. By 2008, the Giants had made it to the championships.

Super Bowl XLII was, at that time, the most-watched Super Bowl and it was that game that really brought Manning into the spotlight. Eli Manning became a household name in America after this game that showcased his inspiring play, his poise and leadership abilities.

The championship was called one of the biggest upsets in Super Bowl history. Everyone predicted that the game would belong to the New England Patriots, who were coming in to the championships with a perfect season. After all, the Giants were the 12-point underdogs and had lost six of their sixteen games in the regular season. It was a bitter outcome for the Patriots, who hadn't been defeated in over a year.

The Giants' game was characterized by a strong defense and an unlikely comeback led by Manning. With just 2:39 remaining on the clock, Manning got the ball in his hands deep in his own territory. Trailing by four, the star quarterback brought his team to victory. He managed to get away from Patriot defenders, heading backwards around the 34-yard line. He threw the ball down the field to David Tyree at the 24-yard line of the Patriots.

Tyree caught the ball in what is now referred to as "The Helmet Catch," initially catching the ball with both hands, but later having to press it against the top of his helmet with one hand. This acrobatic catch gained 32 yards for the Giants, giving them a first down with just 58 seconds left on the clock.

Four plays later, receiver Plaxico Burress managed to score the touchdown that won the Giants the Super Bowl 17-14. Eli Manning threw the 13-yard, Super Bowl-winning touchdown pass to Plaxico Burress to win the game. Notably, it was the third time a touchdown pass in the final minutes ever won a championship game: Layne to Doran in 1953; Montana to Taylor in 1989; and Manning to Burress in 2008.

Manning's reaction to the victory on the field was characterized by his typical reserve. While Giants fans in New York filled Times Square to celebrate, people on highways honked and flashed their lights, and people at home ran out onto the street, Manning was calm, cool and collected. He took the final snap, went down on a knee, got right back up and pumped the ball into the air.

Longtime observers of Manning weren't all too surprised. It was exactly the type of reserve Manning was known for. Later, Manning admitted, "It is hard to explain what that feeling is. You don't know whether to scream or cry or yell. You don't know what to do."

Accorsi, then general manager of the

> "Some of it is genes, a lot of it is just hard work. I never felt pressure. It's just something within yourself that some people have and some people don't. Anything I've ever done, whether it's school or this, I've always worked hard. I don't like doing something halfway."
>
> – Eli Manning

Giants, said it was the greatest night of his career. "It's amazing," Accorsi declared. "Sometimes I have to tangibly remind myself that it happened. You work for your whole career, not only for a championship, but for a quarterback to win a championship – especially me. And then to win it that way? I can't tell you how many times I fantasized and dreamt that was the way it was going to be."

"This team goes nowhere without [Manning]," said Michael Strahan, who saw fifteen NFL seasons before finally getting to his first championship with Manning. Strahan makes no bones about the matter, "This team goes as far as Eli Manning takes us. And Eli Manning has taken us to the Super Bowl. And Eli Manning has won it for us." Unsurprisingly, Manning was named MVP of Super Bowl XLII – just one year after Peyton secured that title in Super Bowl XLI.

2009 Season: Commitments & Changes

In August 2009, Manning signed a six-year, $97.5 million contract extension. The contract guarantees that – barring injury – Manning would be the New York Giants' quarterback until 2015. In return, Manning would be paid a whopping $106.9 million over the next seven years. This total sum includes the $9.4 million he was scheduled to earn in the 2009 season. The contract was tied up for a time, mostly due to conflicting marketing agreements, though both sides insisted that the delay-causing issues were largely inconsequential.

The contract made Manning the eighth member of the $100 million quarterback club – giving him the one up over his brother Peyton, who signed a seven-year, $98 million contract back in 2004. It also put Manning in lead, as the NFL's highest paid player at that time. The contract averaged out to about $15.3 million annually, giving him the highest average annual value of any multi-year contract in NFL history.

Suddenly, in November, just a few months after signing his new contract, Manning faced the reality that he might be out of the game indefinitely. An injury which caused a stress reaction in his foot suddenly put his 2009 season in jeopardy. A reaction in the cuboid bone of Manning's right foot threatened to develop into a stress fracture. This compounded the problem of plantar fasciitis that Manning was struggling with throughout the season, and the pain levels increased dramatically.

After undergoing treatment, Manning was able to play and took particular care to keep the issue under wraps. Some people suspected he did this more to boost the morale of his fellow teammates, as the Giants had been severely affected by injuries and were at the time, on the verge of missing the playoffs.

While the team started the season 5-0, the next eleven games brought them 3-8, securing them a third place finish in the NFC east. The Giants were eliminated from playoff contention in Week 16 in a game against the Carolina Panthers. This would be the last game in the Giants Stadium, before their move to the New

Meadowlands Stadium (now called the MetLife Stadium) which they would continue to share with the New York Jets.

A Dreadful 2010 season

The 2010 season began with the Giants hoping to improve on their 8-8 finish from the previous season, and

> "You are going to have good days and bad days... When you have good days, you play it down and when you have bad games, you have to put it behind you and keep playing. You can't get too high and at the same time you can't get too low."
>
> – Eli Manning

ideally make it to the playoffs after missing postseason. At the start of the 2010 season, things were looking up for Manning, as he had just come off of some career records in terms of completions, completion percentage, passing yards and touchdowns. He also had the opportunity of working with what some observers considered the best young receivers in the NFL: Hakeem Nicks, Steve Smith and Mario Manningham.

However, the 2010 season would have the Giants' star receivers, Nicks and Smith, missing three and seven season games respectively, due to injuries. As for Manningham, he struggled through a concussion, hip and heel injuries throughout the season.

These were just the tip of the iceberg of challenges Manning himself had to face this disastrous season.

Manning certainly didn't shine in the 2010 season, leading the NFL with 25 interceptions, and a quarterback rating of 85.3. This caused many to begin questioning if he even deserved that $97.5 million contract signed just the previous year.

Manning struggled through the season, facing his own slew of injuries, as well as leading the team through the adversity. He ended up throwing 4,002 yards, making 31 touchdowns, completing 62.9 percent of his passes. However, he threw multiple interceptions in eight games, four of which were losses. Shamefully, only in four games in 2010 was Manning interception-free.

NFL Lockout

March 2011 saw the start of a NFL lockout, which barred players from using the facilities and halted league operations. During the lockout, Manning flew under the radar of the media, avoiding making public statements so he wouldn't be quoted saying something inappropriate. No matter what, though, the critics could be counted on to say something about Manning.

Manning's leadership skills were brought to the forefront during the lockout, as he ended up organizing a number of workouts and trainings for team members during the labor unrest. Months before the lockout officially began, Manning was already planning for the delay in spring training, designing workouts for the offensive players and holding them in high schools in his area in New Jersey.

These workouts extended well into the summer, as more and more Giants players gathered for what was christened "Camp Eli." The sessions were organized much like regular practices and offered team members an opportunity to prepare for the regular season.

A Pro's Pro

Despite the media criticism Eli Manning has drawn, whether it is because of his performance on the field or less than charismatic sound bites, it's always been said that Manning is a team player. Right at the start of his career, during training camp back in his first season, the team's assistant equipment manager identified that Manning was a "pro's pro."

Pro Bowl guard Chris Snee commented, "I feel like [Manning] is always being criticized for something. He does a great job of really dealing with everything he is given, He has a lot on his plate as far as what he has to do for our offense, and he does a great job with that. He is always overlooked and never gets the credit he deserves."

Unlike other star quarterbacks, Manning doesn't have the same reputation for having a big ego. While he is proud of the successful plays, he doesn't allow himself to get in the way of the team's performance.

Backup quarterback, David Carr said, "[Manning] does one of the best jobs of putting his ego aside. He takes pride in every play, even a running play. People don't' see that. He wants the perfect angle for every run. He wants to ID the front, so my guys have the best possible play."

Contrary to the "boring" or "standoffish" persona the media tends to portray of Eli Manning, the real man actually has a great sense of humor, pulling pranks and practical jokes, including hiding the center's uniform pants in another team member's locker, spitting sunflower seeds at the center and throwing footballs when they least expect it.

To ease tensions in the midst of the 2011 lockout, Eli joined his brother Peyton in a humorous short video entitled "Football Cops," which was released on DirecTV in late June. It showcased the brothers' acting chops, with the tagline "Nobody escapes the long arms of the law." Equipped with nothing but their famous throwing arms, a couple of footballs and handlebar mustaches, the brothers create a spoof of television crime dramas.

Elite Quarterbacks

> "I never try to be something
> I'm not."
>
> – Eli Manning

In August 2011, Manning gave an interview on The Michael Kay Show, where he declared his top-caliber status. When asked if he believed he was in the same class as three-time Super Bowl champion Tom Brady, Manning was quick to answer, "I consider myself in that class. Tom Brady is a great quarterback, he's a great player and what you've see with him is he's gotten better every year. He started off winning championships and I think he's a better quarterback now than what he was, in all honesty, when he was winning those championships.

"I think now he's grown up and gotten better every year and that's what I'm trying to do. I kind of hope these next seven years of my quarterback days are my best."

Manning's candid answer drew much criticism and derision. Although Manning led the Giants to the playoffs in four of his seven seasons, and even though he did bring the Giants to victory over Tom Brady and the New England Patriots in 2008, observers still didn't place him with the elite quarterbacks.

After all, Tom Brady is a first-ballot Hall of Fame quarterback, as is Eli's older brother, Peyton. Eli Manning's well-known and much-discussed comments also drew scorn as he was just coming out of a pretty poor 2010 season. Critics felt that he would never be able to perform the same way as the other NFL superstars.

Super Bowl 2012

At first, the 2011 season was not looking good for the New York Giants. They were at 7-7, after having lost tragically to the Washington Redskins. Many believed the Giants were too inconsistent to be able to get into the postseason. Surprisingly, after some pivotal wins against the Dallas Cowboys and New York Jets, the Giants came out victorious in the NFC East.

After defeating the Atlanta Falcons, Green Bay Packers and San Francisco 49ers, the Giants had made it as the 2011 NFC champions and were on their way to Indianapolis. They found themselves facing the New England Patriots and Tom Brady, in another final showdown and possibly looking to recoup their loss after Super Bowl XLII.

In the weeks leading up to Super Bowl XLVI, it was clear that in order for the Giants to come out with a victory, Eli Manning needed to bring his game. Could the Giants face their 2008 opponents again and retain their title?

This time around, Manning had the benefit of experience. The last four years had given him a chance to develop his knowledge and strategies, become more aware in the pocket and learn to limit his errors. The championship game was also following the best regular season of Manning's career. He set a career-record high in passing yardage (4,933 yards), which got him the record of fourth highest in the NFL. He also threw a league record 15 touchdown passes in the fourth quarter, bringing the Giants back from fourth quarter deficits six times with his winning drives.

The Giants also enjoyed stronger receivers – Victor Cruz, Hakeem Nicks and Mario Manningham. But would this be enough to beat the Patriots and win what was perhaps the largest Super Bowl rematch in league history? Only time would tell.

February 5, 2012 at the Lucas Oil Stadium, Indianapolis. It was Peyton Manning's city, but it would be Eli's time to shine. While the Patriots won the coin toss, they deferred, and the Giants had first possession. Manning was off to a slow start, but would end up playing a relatively mistake-free game. Early on, Brady started at his own six-yard line and was called for intentional grounding when he sent the ball downfield from the end zone, with no receiver in sight. This put the Giants up 2-0.

The Giants repossessed the ball and went 78 yards in nine plays, Manning passing to Victor Cruz for a two-yard touchdown. They were then up 9-0.

The second quarter of the game saw the Patriots settling for a 29-yard field goal from Stephen Gostkowski, bringing the score up 9-3. However, the Giants retaliated, with Brandown Jacobs converting on a 3rd-and-1. However, a holding call negated the first down, forcing the Giants to punt again.

The Patriots made 14 plays for 99 yards, with Brady throwing a four-yard touchdown pass to Danny Woodhead with just 15 seconds on the clock, bringing the score up 10-9 for the Patriots at halftime.

In the second half of the game, the tides seemed to have turned, as the Patriots were not holding back. The Patriots got possession of the ball first and managed eight plays for 79 yards. Brady threw a second touchdown pass and a twelve-yard strike to tight end Aaron Hernandez, which put the Patriots up 17-9.

Manning brought his A-game and drove the Giants to the twenty-yard line, facilitating a 38-yard field goal for Lawrence Tynes, which brought the score up to 17-12. Next, the Giants brought the ball to the Patriots 15-yard line, setting up a 33-yard field goal for Tynes. At the end of the third quarter, the Patriots were still ahead 17-15.

In the fourth quarter, a missed pass to Wes Welker gave the Giants a big chance to come out ahead. They forced another punt, bringing the ball to their own 12-yard line with only 3:53 on the clock. This was time for Manning to take the lead. The quarterback threw the ball to Mario Manningham, who made a 38-yard catch at the 50-yard line. Manning then made two more passes to Manningham and another the Hakeem Nicks, bringing it down to the 14-yard line. With just 1:04 left in the game, the Giants managed a touchdown, putting them ahead 21-17.

Despite some rallying efforts by the Patriots, including a few ambitious passes by Brady, the score remained at 21-17, the New York Giants once again defeating the New England Patriots in a championship game.

The game opened with Manning becoming the first quarterback to complete his first nine attempts in a championship game. It ended with him directing the nine-play, 88-yard touchdown drive that allowed the Giants to get ahead with just 57 seconds left on the clock. Manning went 30-of-40, with 296 yards and a touchdown, earning him the title of Super Bowl MVP, the second time he's received this award during his career.

His father, Archie Manning commented that he was thoroughly impressed by how Eli reacted during the Giants' championship comeback. He said, "He just hung in there. He was patient, and he had to be patient. He was sacked some early, and it wasn't easy. There wasn't anything easy out there. He played like a quarterback needs to play."

His coach, Tom Coughlin commented, "That was quite a drive that he was able to put together. [Manning] deserves all the credit in the world, because he really has put his team on his shoulders all year."

Off the Field

Manning has been very active in efforts to rebuild New Orleans in the aftermath of Hurricane Katrina. He is also involved in raising awareness regarding the 2010 Gulf oil spill. In addition, he hosts Guiding Eyes for the Blind's Golf Classic, which is a charity event that takes place annually. Manning is also credited with raising $2.5 million which went to the construction of the Eli Manning Children's Clinics at the children's hospital at the University of Mississippi Medical Center.

Shortly after his first Super Bowl triumph, Manning married his college sweetheart during an April 2008 wedding in Los Cabos, Mexico. Eli Manning wed Abby McGrew during a sunset ceremony on the beach, joined by almost 60 friends and family in an intimate wedding at a luxury resort along the Sea of Cortez on the Baja Peninsula.

Conclusion

It's been said that Eli Manning is one of the most overanalyzed, discussed, dissected and criticized quarterback New York has ever had. Some wanted him to be the next Elway. Others thought he was the next Phi Simms. Still others expected that he'd be the next Peyton Manning. It's been a burden Eli Manning has had to bear.

Now that he's beaten the Patriots in not one, but two Super Bowls within a four-year period, Manning has proven that he is in the same class as those other "elite" quarterbacks. It's clear that he's finally ridded himself of the status of "Peyton's younger brother."

All the flak he caught for calling himself an "elite" quarterback seems to have fallen to the wayside. Now that he's got two Super Bowl wins under his belt and just as many championship MVP titles, now that he's defeated Tom Brady twice, both times in fourth-quarter comebacks, and is in his eighth year, it's safe to say that Eli Manning is NFL royalty.

He's got better stats at 30 than Johnny Unitas, Joe Namath and John Elway. Without a doubt, if he keeps going the way he's going, playing just as he's been playing, he can guarantee himself a place in the Hall of Fame. Finally coming into his own, as a quarterback and team leader, Eli Manning and the rest of the world knows that he's entered the world of elite professional quarterbacks.

Stats

College

Year	Att	Comp	Pct	Yds	TD	Int	Rating
2000	53	28	52.8	337	3	2	117.4
2001	408	259	63.5	2,948	31	9	144.8
2002	481	279	58	3,401	21	15	125.6
2003	441	275	62.4	3,600	29	10	148.1
Career	1383	841	61	10,286	84	36	138.1

Professional

2004 REGULAR SEASON GAME LOG

DATE	OPP	RESULT	CMP	ATT	YDS	CMP%	TD	INT	RAT
Sun 9/12	PHI	L 17-31	3	9	66	33.3	0	0	60.4
Sun 11/21	ATL	L 10-14	17	37	162	45.9	1	2	45.1
Sun 11/28	PHI	L 6-27	6	21	148	28.6	0	2	16.9
Sun 12/5	WSH	L 7-31	12	25	113	48	0	0	60.9
Sun 12/12	BAL	L 14-37	4	18	27	22.2	0	2	0
Sat 12/18	PIT	L 30-33	16	23	182	69.6	2	1	103.9
Sun 12/26	CIN	L 22-23	19	37	201	51.4	0	1	56.2
Sun 1/2	DAL	W 28-24	18	27	144	66.7	3	1	101.5
REGULAR SEASON STATS			95	197	1,043	48.2	6	9	55.4

2005 REGULAR SEASON GAME LOG

DATE	OPP	RESULT	CMP	ATT	YDS	CMP %	TD	INT	RAT
Sun 9/11	ARI	W 42-19	10	23	172	43.5	2	2	62.2
Mon 9/19	NO	W 27-10	13	24	165	54.2	1	0	89.8
Sun 9/25	SD	L 23-45	24	41	352	58.5	2	0	102.9
Sun 10/2	STL	W 44-24	19	35	296	54.3	4	0	120.7
Sun 10/16	DAL	L 13-16 (OT)	14	29	215	48.3	1	1	70.3
Sun 10/23	DEN	W 24-23	23	42	214	54.8	2	1	74.9
Sun 10/30	WSH	W 36-0	12	31	146	38.7	1	1	51.3
Sun 11/6	SF	W 24-6	18	33	251	54.5	1	0	89.3
Sun 11/13	MIN	L 21-24	23	48	291	47.9	1	4	39.5
Sun 11/20	PHI	W 27-17	17	26	218	65.4	3	0	130
Sun 11/27	SEA	L 21-24 (OT)	29	53	344	54.7	2	1	79.4
Sun 12/4	DAL	W 17-10	12	31	152	38.7	0	2	27.9
Sun 12/11	PHI	W 26-23 (OT)	28	44	312	63.6	1	3	63.8
Sat 12/17	KC	W 27-17	17	32	186	53.1	1	1	68
Sat 12/24	WSH	L 20-35	23	41	244	56.1	1	1	71.6
Sat 12/31	OAK	W 30-21	12	24	204	50	1	0	93.1
REGULAR SEASON STATS			294	557	3,762	52.8	24	17	75.9

2006 REGULAR SEASON GAME LOG

DATE	OPP	RESULT	CMP	ATT	YDS	CMP%	TD	INT	RAT
Sun 9/10	IND	L 21-26	20	34	247	58.8	2	1	88.7
Sun 9/17	PHI	W 30-24 (OT)	31	43	371	72.1	3	1	111.7
Sun 9/24	SEA	L 30-42	24	36	275	66.7	3	3	82.5
Sun 10/8	WSH	W 19-3	23	33	256	69.7	1	0	102.6
Sun 10/15	ATL	W 27-14	17	30	180	56.7	2	2	68.8
Mon 10/23	DAL	W 36-22	12	26	189	46.2	2	1	80.4
Sun 10/29	TB	W 17-3	16	31	154	51.6	1	0	76.5
Sun 11/5	HOU	W 14-10	17	28	179	60.7	1	1	76.3
Sun 11/12	CHI	L 20-38	14	32	121	43.8	0	2	28.3
Mon 11/20	JAC	L 10-26	19	41	230	46.3	1	2	51.9
Sun 11/26	TEN	L 21-24	18	28	143	64.3	1	2	59.1
Sun 12/3	DAL	L 20-23	24	36	270	66.7	2	0	107.4
Sun 12/10	CAR	W 27-13	17	33	172	51.5	3	0	97
Sun 12/17	PHI	L 22-36	28	40	282	70	0	2	69
Sun 12/24	NO	L 7-30	9	25	74	36	1	1	41.3
Sat 12/30	WSH	W 34-28	12	26	101	46.2	1	0	69.6
REGULAR SEASON STATS			301	522	3,244	57.7	24	18	77

2006 POSTSEASON GAME LOG

DATE	OPP	RESULT	CMP	ATT	YDS	CMP%	TD	INT	RAT
Sun 1/7	PHI	L 20-23	16	27	161	59.3	2	1	85.6
POSTSEASON STATS			16	27	161	59.3	2	1	85.6

2007 REGULAR SEASON GAME LOG

DATE	OPP	RESULT	CMP	ATT	YDS	CMP%	TD	INT	RAT
Sun 9/9	DAL	L 35-45	28	41	312	68.3	4	1	113.1
Sun 9/16	GB	L 13-35	16	29	211	55.2	1	1	75.5
Sun 9/23	WSH	W 24-17	21	36	232	58.3	1	2	63.7
Sun 9/30	PHI	W 16-3	14	26	135	53.8	1	1	65.4
Sun 10/7	NYJ	W 35-24	13	25	186	52	2	1	86.4
Mon 10/15	ATL	W 31-10	27	39	303	69.2	2	2	87.9
Sun 10/21	SF	W 33-15	18	31	146	58.1	2	1	78.2
Sun 10/28	MIA	W 13-10	8	22	59	36.4	0	0	44.9
Sun 11/11	DAL	L 20-31	23	34	236	67.6	1	2	72.7
Sun 11/18	DET	W 16-10	28	39	283	71.8	1	0	100.7
Sun 11/25	MIN	L 17-41	21	49	273	42.9	1	4	33.8
Sun 12/2	CHI	W 21-16	16	27	195	59.3	1	2	63
Sun 12/9	PHI	W 16-13	17	31	219	54.8	1	0	88
Sun 12/16	WSH	L 10-22	18	53	184	34	1	0	51.1
Sun 12/23	BUF	W 38-21	7	15	111	46.7	0	2	32.2
Sat 12/29	NE	L 35-38	22	32	251	68.8	4	1	118.6
REGULAR SEASON STATS			297	529	3,336	56.1	23	20	73.9

2007 POSTSEASON GAME LOG

DATE	OPP	RESULT	CMP	ATT	YDS	CMP%	TD	INT	RAT
Sun 1/6	TB	W 24-14	20	27	185	74.1	2	0	117.1
Sun 1/13	DAL	W 21-17	12	18	163	66.7	2	0	132.4
Sun 1/20	GB	W 23-20 (OT)	21	40	251	52.5	0	0	72
Sun 2/3	NE	W 17-14	19	34	255	55.9	2	1	87.3
POSTSEASON STATS			72	119	854	60.5	6	1	95.7

2008 REGULAR SEASON GAME LOG

DATE	OPP	RESULT	CMP	ATT	YDS	CMP %	TD	INT	RAT
Thu 9/4	WSH	W 16-7	19	35	216	54.3	0	1	61.1
Sun 9/14	STL	W 41-13	20	29	260	69	3	0	131.4
Sun 9/21	CIN	W 26-23 (OT)	26	43	289	60.5	1	0	88.2
Sun 10/5	SEA	W 44-6	19	25	267	76	2	0	136.6
Mon 10/13	CLE	L 14-35	18	28	196	64.3	1	3	57.1
Sun 10/19	SF	W 29-17	16	31	161	51.6	1	0	77.5
Sun 10/26	PIT	W 21-14	19	32	199	59.4	1	0	87.9
Sun 11/2	DAL	W 35-14	16	27	147	59.3	3	1	95.8
Sun 11/9	PHI	W 36-31	17	31	191	54.8	2	1	81.5
Sun 11/16	BAL	W 30-10	13	23	153	56.5	1	1	73.3
Sun 11/23	ARI	W 37-29	26	33	240	78.8	3	0	127.3
Sun 11/30	WSH	W 23-7	21	34	305	61.8	1	1	88.5
Sun 12/7	PHI	L 14-20	13	27	123	48.1	1	0	73.5
Sun 12/14	DAL	L 8-20	18	35	191	51.4	0	2	43.9
Sun 12/21	CAR	W 34-28 (OT)	17	27	181	63	1	0	94.8
Sun 12/28	MIN	L 19-20	11	19	119	57.9	0	0	76.4
REGULAR SEASON STATS			289	479	3,238	60.3	21	10	86.4

2008 POSTSEASON GAME LOG

DATE	OPP	RESULT	CMP	ATT	YDS	CMP%	TD	INT	RAT
Sun 1/11	PHI	L 11-23	15	29	169	51.7	0	2	40.7
POSTSEASON STATS			15	29	169	51.7	0	2	40.7

2009 REGULAR SEASON GAME LOG

DATE	OPP	RESULT	CMP	ATT	YDS	CMP%	TD	INT	RAT
Sun 9/13	WSH	W 23-17	20	29	256	69	1	1	93.5
Sun 9/20	DAL	W 33-31	25	38	330	65.8	2	0	110.6
Sun 9/27	TB	W 24-0	14	24	161	58.3	2	0	106.4
Sun 10/4	KC	W 27-16	20	34	292	58.8	3	1	104
Sun 10/11	OAK	W 44-7	8	10	173	80	2	0	158.3
Sun 10/18	NO	L 27-48	14	31	178	45.2	1	1	61
Sun 10/25	ARI	L 17-24	19	37	243	51.4	1	3	47.5
Sun 11/1	PHI	L 17-40	20	39	222	51.3	1	2	55.7
Sun 11/8	SD	L 20-21	25	33	215	75.8	2	0	112.6
Sun 11/22	ATL	W 34-31 (OT)	25	39	384	64.1	3	1	111.5
Thu 11/26	DEN	L 6-26	24	40	230	60	0	1	65.6
Sun 12/6	DAL	W 31-24	11	25	241	44	2	1	88.9
Sun 12/13	PHI	L 38-45	27	38	391	71.1	3	0	130.5
Mon 12/21	WSH	W 45-12	19	26	268	73.1	3	0	144.4
Sun 12/27	CAR	L 9-41	29	43	296	67.4	1	2	75.3
Sun 1/3	MIN	L 7-44	17	23	141	73.9	0	1	71.1
REGULAR SEASON STATS			317	509	4,021	62.3	27	14	93.1

2010 REGULAR SEASON GAME LOG

DATE	OPP	RESULT	CMP	ATT	YDS	CMP%	TD	INT	RAT
Sun 9/12	CAR	W 31-18	20	30	263	66.7	3	3	87.9
Sun 9/19	IND	L 14-38	13	24	161	54.2	2	1	85.6
Sun 9/26	TEN	L 10-29	34	48	386	70.8	0	2	77.3
Sun 10/3	CHI	W 17-3	18	30	195	60	0	0	79.2
Sun 10/10	HOU	W 34-10	27	42	297	64.3	3	2	89.1
Sun 10/17	DET	W 28-20	20	30	177	66.7	2	0	104.4
Mon 10/25	DAL	W 41-35	25	35	306	71.4	4	3	100.4
Sun 11/7	SEA	W 41-7	21	32	290	65.6	3	0	125.8
Sun 11/14	DAL	L 20-33	33	48	373	68.8	2	2	88.3
Sun 11/21	PHI	L 17-27	20	33	147	60.6	2	3	53.5
Sun 11/28	JAC	W 24-20	14	24	226	58.3	2	0	117.7
Sun 12/5	WSH	W 31-7	15	25	161	60	0	1	62.3
Mon 12/13	MIN	W 21-3	22	37	187	59.5	1	2	59.2
Sun 12/19	PHI	L 31-38	23	39	289	59	4	1	105.6
Sun 12/26	GB	L 17-45	17	33	301	51.5	2	4	63.6
Sun 1/2	WSH	W 17-14	17	29	243	58.6	1	1	83
REGULAR SEASON STATS			339	539	4,002	62.9	31	25	85.3

2011 REGULAR SEASON GAME LOG

DATE	OPP	RESULT	CMP	ATT	YDS	CMP%	TD	INT	RAT
Sun 9/11	WSH	L 14-28	18	32	268	56.3	0	1	70.8
Mon 9/19	STL	W 28-16	19	30	223	63.3	2	1	94.2
Sun 9/25	PHI	W 29-16	16	23	254	69.6	4	0	145.7
Sun 10/2	ARI	W 31-27	27	40	321	67.5	2	0	108.4
Sun 10/9	SEA	L 25-36	24	39	420	61.5	3	3	91.8
Sun 10/16	BUF	W 27-24	21	32	292	65.6	0	0	94.8
Sun 10/30	MIA	W 20-17	31	45	349	68.9	2	0	106.6
Sun 11/6	NE	W 24-20	20	39	250	51.3	2	1	77.9
Sun 11/13	SF	L 20-27	26	40	311	65	2	2	84.5
Sun 11/20	PHI	L 10-17	18	35	264	51.4	1	1	74
Mon 11/28	NO	L 24-49	33	47	406	70.2	2	1	101.9
Sun 12/4	GB	L 35-38	23	40	347	57.5	3	1	100.7
Sun 12/11	DAL	W 37-34	27	47	400	57.4	2	1	90.7
Sun 12/18	WSH	L 10-23	23	40	257	57.5	0	3	45.5
Sat 12/24	NYJ	W 29-14	9	27	225	33.3	1	1	61.5
Sun 1/1	DAL	W 31-14	24	33	346	72.7	3	0	136.7
REGULAR SEASON STATS			359	589	4,933	61	29	16	92.9

2011 POSTSEASON GAME LOG

DATE	OPP	RESULT	CMP	ATT	YDS	CMP%	TD	INT	RAT
Sun 1/8	ATL	W 24-2	23	32	277	71.9	3	0	129.3
Sun 1/15	GB	W 37-20	21	33	330	63.6	3	1	114.5
Sun 1/22	SF	W 20-17 (OT)	32	58	316	55.2	2	0	82.3
Sun 2/5	NE	W 21-17	30	40	296	75	1	0	103.8
POSTSEASON STATS			106	163	1,219	65	9	1	103.3

Made in the USA
Monee, IL
27 January 2020